# FROM FEAR to FAITH

# From Fear to Faith

## J. KLENK

TRISTAN PUBLISHING

MINNEAPOLIS

Library of Congress Cataloging-in-Publication Data

Names: Klenk, Julie, author.
Title: From fear to faith / written by Julie Klenk.
Description: Golden Valley : TRISTAN Publishing, 2019.
Identifiers: LCCN 2018036136 | ISBN 9781939881182 (pbk.)
Subjects: LCSH: Fear—Religious aspects—Christianity. | Anxiety—Religious
aspects—Christianity. | Devotional exercises.
Classification: LCC BV4908.5 .K56 2019 | DDC 248.8/6—dc23
LC record available at https://lccn.loc.gov/2018036136

TRISTAN Publishing, Inc.
2355 Louisiana Avenue North
Golden Valley, MN  55427

ISBN 978-1-939881-18-2
Printed in the USA
First Printing

To learn more about all of our books with a message,
visit us at www.TRISTANpublishing.com

# TABLE OF CONTENTS

*To everyone who has ever sat with me over the years and shared your story at Dunn Brothers, Caribou, Starbucks, church, or my kitchen—this study came through you! Thank you for trusting me and letting me into your world. You are braver than you think. Your fears and struggles and pain inspired me to pursue the Lord and discover His plan for us in the midst of the storms.*

*To my Emma Rose—this has been a part of your story. I have watched you live this out through each challenge He has put before you. You are a strong, beautiful woman of faith! I love you!*

*~J.*

# INTRODUCTION

My journey from fear to faith began many years ago. As a young parent, I lived in fear and worry about everything in this crazy world. How could I keep my kids safe and shield them from this awful place? Worn out and exhausted from the stress, I thought it was a normal response to life. One afternoon a friend and I walked along the beach, talking about the difficulties of life. She wore a necklace that had belonged to her mother—the pendant, a tiny mustard seed. That seemingly insignificant seed captured my attention. There wasn't much to it, and yet it pointed to something much greater. A little seed of faith has powerful, even miraculous results. The seed prompted me to begin praying and trusting God in mighty ways—for my family, my fears and my worries. Who knew where that mustard seed would lead me?

Fast forward a lot of years, and I will say that this world has become even crazier. So much in life can cause us to fear. At our fingertips we constantly have access to the latest headlines—natural disasters, shootings, political tensions, terrorism, and diseases. Add to that the stress in our personal lives— jobs, marriage, children, illness—and it's no wonder that more and more people are diagnosed with anxiety disorders. Life is stressful. It can fill us with fear. So how do we go from living a life of fear . . . to living a life of faith? It really is one step at a time, a process. God wants to do something deep within each of us, to move us out of our fears and into a place of deeper trust in Him. He is, of course, able to deliver us from our fears at any moment, but I do believe that, for most of us, He doesn't miraculously make our fears go away. Instead, He guides us through the process of growing our faith. He teaches us how to renew our minds. He grows the root of faith deep so that—no matter what comes our way— we'll know how to respond. Oh, how good He is to us!

This study is really about taking one step at a time. Imagine this little book as the instructions for growing a beautiful garden. Your soul is that garden. It's trying to be fruitful, but maybe the worries and cares of this world are choking out the fruit. God sees you and knows exactly where you are . . . and He knows exactly how to grow faith in you.

In each of the next twelve weeks, we'll focus on a specific way to apply the Word of God to our lives as we move from fear to faith. We'll need to dig out the weeds of fear, plant the seed of faith, and learn how to nourish and protect that seed as it sprouts. As we continue the study, we'll watch new growth take place and see the fruit in our lives. It will be exciting! Remember, a garden doesn't grow overnight. God is patient in the process, and He promises to be with us each step of the way. I'm praying that the Holy Spirit will encourage your heart as you begin taking one step at a time! Who knows where that little seed of faith will lead you?

# DIG OUT WEEDS

## WEEK 1

The first step we need to take in moving from fear to faith is to examine the state of our hearts. The very first garden mentioned in the Bible was the Garden of Eden. It was perfect, filled with good things, and Adam and Eve were given the role of caretakers. Since the beginning of time God has given us responsibilities. In Proverbs, we see a very different picture of a garden.

> I passed by the field of the sluggard
>
> And by the vineyard of the man lacking sense,
>
> And behold, it was completely overgrown with thistles;
>
> Its surface was covered with nettles,
>
> And its stone wall was broken down.
>
> When I saw, I reflected upon it;
>
> I looked and received instruction.
>
> —Proverbs 24:30–32

This garden was a disaster. Thorns and nettles had overtaken the field and vineyard. The owner had neglected his property. The stone wall that was meant to protect the garden was falling apart, and everything was in ruins. Solomon tells us that he saw it, he reflected, and he learned something from this scene. He observed that someone was not taking care of what was entrusted to him. God has a purpose for each of our lives, and we need to be good stewards of the time on earth He has entrusted to us.

Maybe your life is overwhelmed with worries and fears, and it resembles this garden. All you can see are the ruins. Or maybe your garden is looking pretty good, but you do have a few nettles poking out. It doesn't matter if your garden is in a bad state. God desires to help you clean it up. He's not going to do it all for us, but He would love to help! Weeds will take over a garden if we neglect to dig them out. The same is true for our souls. If we neglect to deal with sin, it will crowd out all the good things we are trying to grow.

Weeds are invasive. They're undesirable and harmful. If we allow them to grow in our lives, there will be less space for fruit. Weeds grow really fast. If you're a gardener, you know that you have to stay on top of the weeds or they'll quickly overtake your garden. Fear is like a weed, and it makes a mess of our lives. It's hard to be fruitful when we are fearful. I once planted a large portion of my yard with wildflowers. The trouble with wildflowers is that it's hard to tell which one is a weed and which is a flower. Some of my "flowers" grew to five feet tall, sprinkled with the tiniest of flowers and covered with nettles. It seemed like a daunting task to begin cleaning up my garden. The same is true for our lives. It's work—and it can even be painful to pull out the weeds, but they must go in order to grow the seed of faith. Moving from fear to faith is hard work. During our study we'll look at why fear sometimes grows in our lives. There might be something that we don't believe about God or His promises.

In the Proverbs scripture, we saw that there was a garden that needed care. Similarly, God has given each of us a life; the care of it is our responsibility. We need to be diligent in cultivating and caring for our souls so that the seed of faith can grow. This requires action. As we go through this week's lesson, we'll learn that before we can plant the seed of faith, we need to dig out the weeds of fear.

## DAY 1

Everyone deals with fear or worry in their lives. Many are tossed in every which direction, and it seems that fear has the upper hand. Others have learned to navigate the storms and challenges of life quite well. Some are well aware of what causes their fears and worries, while others cannot pinpoint that unsettled feeling. Sometimes we refer to fear and worry with more acceptable terms. We use terms such as *fret, concern, overthinking, losing sleep over, stress* . . . As we learn to dig out the weeds of fear, we need to identify our fears.

What words do you use to describe your fears and worries in life?

_____

_____

_____

Each week we will memorize a key verse or two to help us focus on the week's lesson. When we memorize Scripture, the Holy Spirit will bring the passage to our minds to comfort us and encourage us when we need it. Our memory verse this week is Psalm 56:3. Are you worried that you can't memorize Scripture? Before you begin, pray and ask the Holy Spirit to help you. He is, after all, our Helper!

Write out Psalm 56:3.

_____

_____

_____

The fact is, we will have storms in life that could cause us to fear and worry. In Psalm 56:3, David gives us the battle plan to deal with fear. On a separate sheet of paper, make a list of all the fears and worries you have right now. If you are stumped at articulating what your fears might be, think about what preoccupies your thoughts or keeps you awake at night. Pray and ask the Holy Spirit to show you your fears and worries. After you've completed your list, spend time thanking the Lord for what He has shown you. Your list might be overwhelming to you, but it's not to God!

## DAY 2

Challenging and difficult times are part of life. Fear is a God-given emotion that can protect us, which is a good thing! But if we don't know how to deal with fear, it can overtake us, which isn't a good thing! The Bible is filled with passages that tell us not to fear or worry. God is not saying we should never experience fear. He is saying we need to avoid letting fear overtake us. From this week's memory verse, we learn to take our fears to the Lord. When we do that, we're saying that we won't stay stuck in fear because we know that the Lord is able to handle whatever storms we experience. Worry is like fear on steroids. It grows out of control. It can overtake us and paralyze us. Worry is taking our eyes off Jesus and entertaining all the *what ifs* spinning through our minds. God calls us to believe that He is who He says He is—and that He will do what He says He will do. When we choose not to believe God's truth, this is unbelief and it is sin.

Spend time now going through your list of fears and worries. Pray and ask the Holy Spirit to show you what it is that you don't believe about God or His promises; then write down next to each fear what you struggle to believe. In our memory verse, David tells us that instead of staying stuck in fear, he will put his trust in the Lord. Trust begins when we give our fears and worries to the Lord. He never expects us to figure them out or handle them on our own.

In order to get rid of weeds, we need to dig out the roots. We do this by admitting that our fears and worries are sin because of our unbelief that God will be faithful to His promises. Go through your list and confess to the Lord that you have sinned by letting fear and worry take over your heart instead of trusting in Him and His promises.

What does 1 John 1:9 promise us?

_____

_____

_____


Confessing our sins to the Lord pulls out that weed of fear in our lives; it's the first step. As we go through the study, we'll learn how to keep those weeds from coming back. Spend time thanking the Lord for His forgiveness that makes us clean and gives us a fresh start!

## DAY 3

Unbelief will sprout the weed of fear. When you recognize that you don't believe God or His promises, you need to confess it as sin so God is able to come into your situation and provide. Pray and ask the Holy Spirit to teach you as you read through the lesson today.

Read Mark 4:35–41.

What were the disciples facing?

What did they think was going to happen?

In verse 38, the disciples asked Jesus a question. Have you ever been in a storm of life, or are you in one now—and asking Him a similar question? Describe that storm.

According to the book of Luke, this storm took place at the end of the second year of Jesus' ministry. The disciples had been with Jesus for almost two years, and they had witnessed many miracles. However, in that storm they doubted God's promises—doubted that He cared for them, which was unbelief. No matter how long you've known the Lord and no matter what you've seen Him do, you may be tempted to fear and worry unless you trust Him and His promises.

After Jesus took care of the storm, He asked the disciples in verse 40, "Why are you afraid? Do you still have no faith?" What was Jesus saying to them?

Should we fear our storms, or should we fear the One who has authority over our storms?

Was it encouraging to discover that even the disciples struggled with fear and unbelief?

Spend time praying through your list of fears and worries with the Lord. As you do, declare that He is Lord over those fears and worries in your life.

## DAY 4

Today we are going to read Psalm 56 and discover what was going on in David's life at the time. In order to understand this psalm, read 1 Samuel 21:10–15. David was attempting to escape King Saul, who was trying to kill him. As if that wasn't bad enough, David was then captured by the Philistines in Gath. (Remember, David had killed the big Philistine Goliath—the Philistines were thrilled to capture him.) After David's release, he was still in a rather bad situation, and it was then that he wrote Psalm 56.

Pray and ask the Holy Spirit to teach you as you read Psalm 56.

In verses 1 and 2 David describes his situation. What was he facing?

_____

_____

How was he feeling?

_____

_____

I hope you noticed in these verses that David confessed or admitted exactly how he felt. He didn't deny his feelings. When we're faced with worries and fears, we need to be honest before the Lord.

Look at verses 3 and 4. How did David handle his fears?

_____

_____

David knew that God had anointed him to be the next king. His situation could have convinced him otherwise. David chose to trust God and His promises. What did David know about God in verses 8 and 9?

_____

_____

Do you believe that God is always for you? If so, give examples from your own life. If not, why, and how could life be better if you believed it?

_____

_____

When David was afraid, he put his trust in God. David knew that God was faithful to His promises. Spend time in prayer thanking the Lord that He sees exactly where you are on this journey. Thank Him that He is for you!

# DAY 5

When we read through the Scriptures, we can see all the promises that God has for us. This is exciting! However, sometimes we can miss out on our part of the equation before God answers His promises. As we've learned this week, digging out the weeds is our responsibility. There is work that we must do and then the Lord is faithful to do His part.

Write out the following verses. In each verse is a command and a promise. Underline the command (our responsibility) and double underline the promise (God's responsibility).

Joshua 1:9

_____

_____

_____

Isaiah 41:10

_____

_____

_____

1 John 1:9

_____

_____

_____

The Lord himself is walking with you through the storms of life. Spend time committing to the Lord your desire to obey His commands to not fear or worry. Ask the Holy Spirit to help you obey and to remind you to confess when you have not. Thank the Lord that He is faithful to help you on this journey . . . and He will help you move from fear to faith!

# LOOK UP

Growing a garden takes time; it's a process. I was a preschool teacher for 20 years, and I learned that God is a lot like a preschool teacher. He has a lot of children, and He's all about the process! When the first snowfall came each year, I would teach eighteen two-year-olds how to get their snow clothes on. It was a process! I was there to watch and help, but I would not do their job. On our journey from fear to faith, God is our Teacher; He's watching over us, He will help us along the way, but He will not do things that He has equipped us to do. There is an order to getting snow clothes on. It isn't possible to pull snow pants on over shoes, first the shoes must come off. And so it is with faith. Before we could plant the seed of faith, we needed to clear the weeds out; and now we need to prepare the soil. We do this by renewing our minds in His Word; this is where transformation takes place. It is a process!

One of my favorite hobbies is horseback riding. My favorite horse is a Clydesdale that weighs 1,850 pounds. She is strong, enthusiastic, and easily distracted. Often, you'll see these giant draft horses with blinders over their eyes. Blinders help them to focus on what is ahead rather than what is at the side or behind. Blinders prevent distraction and panic. This week we will study the character of God so we can know Him better and trust Him more. As we put our blinders on, we will be focused on Him and not resort to panic!

We often use words like *omnipotent*, *omniscient*, and *omnipresent* to describe God. Do we understand what those words mean, and do we really believe they are true about God? When I taught those precious preschoolers, I had no trouble getting them to believe we serve a mighty God. They believe in God with their sweet, childlike faith. They boldly declared how powerful and amazing God is. Oh, if we could only keep that perspective throughout our lives! God does not change. He is still powerful and amazing! As we grow older, hard times come and we may get distracted and less enthusiastic about our relationship with God. We look at our circumstances and start to doubt God's goodness, His faithfulness, and His love. We forget who He really is. In the book of Psalms, we get a glimpse of how mighty God is.

The Lord is high above all nations;

His glory is above the heavens.

Who is like the Lord our God,

Who is enthroned on high,

Who humbles Himself to behold

The things that are in heaven and in the earth?

He raises the poor from the dust

And lifts the needy from the ash heap,

To make them sit with princes,

With the princes of His people.

He makes the barren woman abide in the house

As a joyful mother of children.

Praise the Lord!

—Psalm 113:4–9

This psalm gives us an idea of the greatness of our God. We learn that the Lord is high above all the nations, and His glory is above the heavens. God is transcendent—He exists above and beyond the created universe. He is completely set apart from His creatures and His creation. This is our BIG God! There is no one like our God, no one even comes close. Can I just say that there is not a better solution to your fears and worries than our amazing God? Although God is exalted on high, He descends to meet the needy. In our fears and worries, we are the needy! God is concerned for the poor, the needy and the barren woman. He is also concerned for the fearful and the worriers. He is compassionate toward those who are broken. Our God is all knowing, always with us, and all powerful—and He comes down to us right where we are. This should bless our hearts! Our God, who is above all things, is for us!

## DAY 1

We have already removed some weeds of fear by confessing our unbelief. Now we prepare the ground before the seed of faith is planted. For our faith to grow, we need to trust the Lord. This week we'll spend some time in the Word looking at who God says He is. We'll find that He is worthy of our faith. Before you begin to memorize your verse this week, pray and ask the Holy Spirit to help you.

Write out our memory verses for this week, Psalm 121:1–2.

_____

_____

_____

When you struggle with fear and worry, where will your help come from?

_____

_____

_____

What do you learn about God in verse 2?

_____

_____

_____

The One who made all things is ready to help us when we look to Him. These verses are a powerful declaration. When we speak them, we are turning our eyes from our fears to the One who is over all our fears. Whatever the storm or challenge you face, look up to Him and seek His help. Our help in going from fear to faith will come from the Lord. Spend time praying through your list of fears and worries, and declare to the Lord that—in each situation—He is your help.

## DAY 2

When we look up to the Lord, we find that He is so much more than we can think or imagine! In the presence of the Lord, our worries and fears shrink. To trust God, we need to know His character. The next two days we will look in the Word to see some of God's attributes. The more we know Him, the more we can trust Him. Pray and ask the Holy Spirit to impress on your heart who God really is. Read the following verses and write down who God is and what He will do for those who look to Him.

Genesis 22:13–14

Exodus 3:14

Deuteronomy 7:9

Nehemiah 9:6

Job 36:5

Psalm 18:2

Psalm 46:1

Psalm 75:7

Psalm 86:15

Psalm 139:7–12

As you look at your list of fears and worries, do any of these passages bring you hope that He can comfort and help you? Spend time in prayer thanking Him for who He is, and that He is more than able to handle your fears and worries.

## DAY 3

As you continue to look through the Scriptures today, pray and ask the Holy Spirit to teach you more about God's character. Write down who God is and what He will do for those who look to Him.

Psalm 147:5

Isaiah 9:6

Isaiah 44:24

Lamentations 3:22–23

Zephaniah 3:17

Matthew 14:14

_____

_____

Matthew 19:26

_____

_____

John 3:16

_____

_____

Jude 1:24–25

_____

_____

After reading these verses, do you have a better understanding of how great our God is? In what ways does this list encourage you that God can handle all your fears and worries?

_____

_____

Spend time in prayer looking up to the Lord Most High. Thank Him for who He is and that He is above all your fears and worries.

# DAY 4

Today we are going to read and meditate on Psalm 121. What does it mean to meditate on God's Word?

_____

_____

_____

Meditating on the Word is more than just reading the passage. It is a process. Meditating requires us to read and reread a passage. Then, we quiet our hearts and ask the Holy Spirit to speak to us through God's Word. We might need to define words to get a better understanding of what the passages mean. We ponder how it applies to our lives. Next, we put it into action. It becomes a part of us, not just a passage that we read but can't recall a few hours later.

Psalm 121 is called A Song of Ascents. This was a song the Jewish people sang as they headed up the mountains to Jerusalem for the annual feasts of Passover and Booths. Meditate on the following verses and write down what the psalmist is telling us about the Lord. Pray and ask the Holy Spirit to help you.

Verses 1–2:

_____

_____

Verses 3–4:

_____

_____

Verses 5–6:

_____

_____

Verses 7–8:

Looking at these passages, how can you apply them to your fears and worries? Spend time praying through your fears and worries while declaring that He is able to help you in each situation.

# DAY 5

Pray and ask the Holy Spirit to teach you as you again read about the storm on the sea, this time from Luke 8:22–25.

In verse 22, Jesus tells the disciples they were all going over to the other side of the Sea of Galilee. Jesus knew they were actually going to get to the other side.

Does God know the storm you are experiencing and how long it will last? Does He know the storms you'll face in the future?

_____

_____

_____

Does He know how to take care of you in those storms?

_____

_____

_____

What did Jesus do after the disciples woke him?

_____

_____

_____

Explain what happened in verse 25.

_____

_____

This was a different kind of fear. This was an understanding that God is much bigger than they had thought. Are you recognizing that He is much greater than you think?

Read Revelation 1:17. Sometimes we forget how holy and mighty God is. Those who witnessed His glory responded in fear—not a cowering fear, but a reverential awe of Him! We need to remember who God really is.

Write out Proverbs 3:7–8. Underline the command and double underline the promise.

Spend time in prayer thanking God that He is so much bigger than we could think or imagine—and yet He meets us right where we are! Ask Him to help you continue to look up to Him in each fear and worry.

# CHOOSE FAITH

## WEEK 3

Everyone lives by faith. The question is, in whom or what are we placing our faith? Some people place their faith in themselves or others. Some have faith in their jobs, governments, or stocks and investments. At some point, their faith will crumble because these are not worthy faith objects. We need someone or something that is worthy of our faith. We lifted our eyes to the hills and found that our help comes from the Lord. We studied some characteristics of God, and we discovered that He is above everything . . . and He alone is trustworthy. The more we know God, the more we can put our trust in Him. He will not fail us.

Fear leaves us stuck, but faith moves us forward. In our garden, fear makes it look as if the weeds have taken over so nothing else will grow. Faith looks at the garden and sees the possibility, not only for new growth, but for fruit. Faith in Jesus will change our lives. He is all about new life and new growth. God is the master gardener who knows just how to accomplish this in each one of us!

> "For truly I say to you, if you have faith the size of a mustard seed, you will say to this mountain, 'Move from here to there,' and it will move; and nothing will be impossible to you."
> —Matthew 17:20

I love Jesus' words *if you have faith the size of a mustard seed*. Did you know the mustard seed is one of the smallest seeds? It seems quite insignificant, but according to this verse, great and mighty things can happen when we have a tiny bit of faith! Faith doesn't start out big; it starts out small and grows. Every time we choose faith instead of fear or worry, we nourish that little seed.

The mustard seed really is quite fascinating. Although it's one of the tiniest seeds, it grows quickly—and to immense proportions. A mustard plant can be twenty feet tall and twenty feet wide. Do not become discouraged in this process of moving from fear to faith! God can grow us quickly. The mustard plant, which looks more like a tree, cannot be easily blown over. This is so exciting! When our faith grows, our fears and worries can no longer blow us over!

Maybe you're in a season of intense pruning. I've got good news for you! If a mustard plant is cut down to the trunk, it will grow and come back stronger. In challenging times, it feels as if we won't rise again. Fear keeps us in that spot, but faith is what allows us to overcome—and even come back stronger.

This week we'll see we *choose* to have faith. It's our responsibility to plant the seed of faith in our gardens. God will help us. The fears in our lives might look impossible or immovable; but when we choose faith, we are declaring that God is who He says He is—and He will do what He says He will do!

# DAY 1

We have dug out the weeds of fear and prepared our hearts with a right perspective of who God is, and now it is time to plant the seed of faith. How would you define faith?

_____

_____

_____

Write out our memory verse this week, Hebrews 11:6. Pray and ask the Holy Spirit to help you learn the verse each week!

_____

_____

_____

_____

_____

According to our verse, how important is it to live by faith in Christ?

_____

_____

_____

The seed of faith is tiny, but it can take root and grow quickly! Spend time praying through your list of fears and worries, declaring that you will choose by faith to believe that God is who He says He is—and He will do what He says He will do.

## DAY 2

Do you know anyone who lives out their faith? Describe what you see in that person's life.

Every giant tree began in the same way—as a little seed. Our faith doesn't start out big. God grows it one challenge, one fear, one trial, one worry at a time. Pray and ask the Holy Spirit to teach you as you read Hebrews 11.

What key phrase is repeated throughout the passage?

"By faith" is choosing to believe God is who He says he is—and that He will do what He says He will do.

What is faith according to verse 1?

Write out some of the challenges these saints were facing.

These saints did not have the promises that we have in Christ. They chose to place their faith in God and trust Him. What do we learn in verses 39–40?

They did not receive all that was promised. They did not live to see the Messiah in flesh. They obtained the promise in heaven. When Christ came, He fulfilled the promise. We get to experience the promise now and in eternity! Jesus is the promise and the answer to all our fears and worries. Spend time thanking Him that He is what you need, and He will meet your needs in the midst of your fears and worries.

## DAY 3

Ask the Holy Spirit to teach you as you read and meditate on Psalm 27. Remember to meditate on the Scripture. Sometimes we can be in such a rush to get to the answers that we forget to sit and reflect on what God is showing us.

Who is the Lord in verse 1?

_____

_____

_____

What is David saying in verse 3?

_____

_____

_____

How can you be confident despite your trials?

_____

_____

It's okay if you're not there yet! Don't worry! God will grow your faith deep as you learn to choose Him.

Verses 4–6 talk about being in the presence of the Lord. What happens when we seek Him and spend time with Him?

_____

_____

_____

When we're in His presence, there is no room for fear! Instead, we are in awe of Him, comforted and protected by Him. What a great place to be!

Write out verse 14.

_____

_____

_____

_____

When we wait for the Lord, we are choosing by faith to believe He will move on our behalf. Thank Him that He will help you through this whole process of moving from fear to faith.

# DAY 4

Today we're going to look at another stormy-sea situation. Pray and ask the Holy Spirit to help you understand.

Read Matthew 14:22–33. Summarize what is happening during this boat ride.

_____

_____

_____

Why were the disciples afraid in verse 26?

_____

_____

How did Jesus respond?

_____

_____

Peter was the brave one of the group. In verse 29, what did Peter choose by faith to do? How did that work for him?

_____

_____

What happened in verse 30?

_____

_____

What happens when you look at your situation or your fears instead of looking at Jesus?

_____

_____

The good news is that if we cry out to Him, He will respond just as He did for Peter. Spend time in prayer crying out to Him and asking for His help in your fears and storms. Thank Him that He never gives up on you!

## DAY 5

Faith is a choice. In every fear or worry, we have a choice to make. By faith you can choose to believe that God is true to His Word and faithful to you—or you can choose to focus on your situation and miss Him altogether.

Write out the following verses. Underline the command and double underline the promise.

Proverbs 3:5–6

_____

_____

_____

Psalm 9:9–10

_____

_____

_____

Psalm 84:11–12

_____

_____

_____

Trusting in the Lord is choosing faith. The Lord rewards those who seek Him! Make these verses your prayer to the Lord. Personalize them as you pray. Ask the Lord to grow your little seed of faith!

# WORSHIP HIM

## WEEK 4

The first thing that happens to a seed after it has been planted is that it grows roots. This all takes place hidden underground. We might not yet see what God is doing in us through this study, but He is doing something. Keep persevering! When the roots take hold, the plant will begin to grow. As the plant grows, it will be nourished by nutrients in the soil. Over the course of this study we'll look at different disciplines that will nourish our little plants of faith. Not only will these disciplines feed our faith, they will also protect it.

A very important way to feed our faith is to worship the Lord. The more we worship the Lord and acknowledge His greatness, the more our faith increases. The more our faith increases, the more we want to worship the Lord! In Hebrew the word *worship* means to bow down. Bowing is lowering ourselves before the Lord. It is surrendering. When we worship the Lord, we stop resisting Him. Worship is so much more than a lip response to the Lord, it is a heart response that says He is God and I am not. He alone is to be worshiped.

> For you shall not worship any other god,
> for the Lord, whose name is Jealous, is a jealous God.
> —Exodus 34:14

Worshiping the Lord is much more than singing on a Sunday morning. We worship the Lord with our bodies, our hearts, our minds, and our will. In all that we do, we are called to worship Him. The logical time to worship and praise the Lord is when everything is going well in our lives—when there has been victory and we feel like singing. However, great power comes in worshiping the Lord in the battle, the storm, or the fear. It is a challenge to worship the Lord when everything seems wrong, but when we choose to worship Him, everything changes. We will find that our hearts and minds are refreshed, encouraged, and strengthened by a right perspective of Him. When He is magnified, everything else in our lives looks less threatening.

God is above all that we know or understand. What fear or worry are you in right now? He is over all those fears and worries. He understands and sees what we cannot see. He is worthy to be praised! He is exalted above any fear—any storm that we are walking in right now, and the ones that we have yet to face. Worshiping the Lord is a safe place to be, everything changes when we fix our eyes on Jesus. Did you know that joy is a natural result of spending time with the Lord? Joy is not about happy and pleasant circumstances, joy is about the Lord. The joy of the Lord is our strength. When we worship the Lord, we receive joy and strength for whatever we face!

## DAY 1

We worship the Lord because He is worthy of all praise and honor. In the midst of our fears and trials, worship is a powerful tool that lifts our eyes off ourselves and our struggles and onto Him. Our hearts and minds are comforted when we worship Him for who He is.

Write out our memory verse this week, Psalm 95:6.

What does it mean to worship the Lord?

Pray and ask the Holy Spirit to teach you about worship as you read and meditate on Psalm 95. What commands are we given in these passages?

Why?

The psalmist tells us in verses 7–8 that if we hear His voice, we are not to harden our hearts. To hear His voice means to listen to what the Lord commands us in Scripture—and then obey. When we do this, our hearts remain soft for the Lord.

Verses 9–11 are a warning to us. The Israelites were not allowed into the land of rest because of their unbelief. When we disobey the Lord's commands, we miss out on the rest He has for us. Listening to His voice with a heart to obey Him and trust in His promises is a sure way to find our rest in Him! Spend time worshiping the Lord for who He is.

## DAY 2

Pray and ask the Holy Spirit to teach you as you read John 4:1–42.

In verses 21–22, Jesus told the Samaritan woman something important about worship. What was it?

_____

_____

In verses 23–24, what does He say true worship is?

_____

_____

What does it mean to worship God in spirit and in truth?

_____

_____

_____

Jesus wants our worship to come from the heart. When we understand who God really is, we will treasure Him above all other things.

What does worshiping the Lord look like in your life?

_____

_____

In verse 26, what does the woman at the well learn?

_____

_____

What does she do with that information?

_____

_____

What happened as a result of her worshiping the Lord, according to verses 39–42?

_____

_____

When we are worshiping the Lord in spirit and in truth, how does it affect our list of fears and worries?

_____

_____

Spend time worshiping the Lord and make the choice to treasure Him above all other things.

# DAY 3

Today we're going to dig into the Old Testament to see how worship was a powerful tool in the midst of trouble. Pray and ask the Holy Spirit to teach you as you read 2 Chronicles 20:1–12.

At this time in history, Israel was divided into two kingdoms. Israel was the northern kingdom and Judah the southern kingdom. King Jehoshaphat reigned in the South, which included Jerusalem.

What was reported to Jehoshaphat in verse 2? How did he take that news, according to verses 3–4?

_____

_____

_____

Jehoshaphat stood before the assembly and began worshiping the Lord. From verses 6 to 11, write out a few examples of what he was declaring about God.

_____

_____

_____

Jehoshaphat had a right understanding of who God was. A great multitude was coming to invade. He could have readied the troops, drawn up the battle plans, and taken control of His kingdom, but instead he turned to God first! When the battles come to your life, where do you usually turn first?

_____

_____

_____

I love verse 12! Jehoshaphat sums up the situation to the Lord—and what does he declare?

_____

_____

I am certain that the Lord was delighted to hear that, even though they had no idea what to do, their eyes were on Him!!! When our eyes are on Him, the Lord will always respond. He is faithful!

Spend time in prayer worshiping the Lord and declaring that your eyes are on Him through each of your fears and worries.

# DAY 4

Pray and ask the Holy Spirit to help you understand as we finish reading the story in 2 Chronicles 20:13–30.

What was the message the Lord gave to the assembly through Jahaziel?

_____

_____

In verses 18–19, how did the people respond?

_____

_____

Had the victory actually come by then?

_____

_____

By faith they chose to worship the Lord *ahead* of the victory. This is important!

In verses 20–23, we see the game plan unfold. In verse 20 what did Jehoshaphat exhort his people to do?

_____

_____

_____

Whom did he send out before the army?

_____

_____

What happened when they began to sing and praise the Lord?

_____

_____

If we want God to show up, we need to begin worshiping Him.

Summarize verses 24–30.

_____

_____

_____

_____

There was quite a bit of worshiping going on in this story. The assembly worshiped the Lord as the battle was coming. They worshiped the Lord during the battle, believing He was going to do something. They worshiped the Lord when victory finally came.

Spend time worshiping the Lord, thanking Him that He is bigger than your list of fears and worries. Declare to Him your desire to worship Him when you see new storms coming, when you are in the middle of them, and when victory comes!

# DAY 5

Psalm 34 is one of thanksgiving that David wrote after the Lord delivered him. Pray and ask the Holy Spirit for help as you read and meditate on Psalm 34.

According to verse 1, when should we worship the Lord?

_____

_____

Write out Psalm 34:4. Underline the command and double underline the promise.

_____

_____

What do you need to do before the Lord answers?

_____

_____

There are so many exciting truths and promises in Psalm 34! Write down some of the verses that really encourage your heart. How do they bring you hope?

_____

_____

When we are worshiping the Lord with a right understanding of who He is, we will be delivered from all our fears. Don't worry or be discouraged, it's a process! Spend time right now worshiping Him. He will do His part.

# DESTROY IDOLS

## WEEK 5

Sometimes we feel that our needs or desires are not being met by God, and we turn to something else to satisfy us. Something or someone we knowingly—or unknowingly—place above God is an idol. It's easy to think of idols as bad things that pull us away from God, but even good things like our marriage, family, children, and jobs can become idols. Idols can be people—celebrities, athletes, politicians, a spouse, children . . . Idols can be possessions—houses, cars, iPhones, money . . . Idols can be activities—sports, hobbies, Facebook, Twitter . . . Idols can be goals or desires—good health, a perfect marriage, obedient children, wealth, reputation, being in control . . . Whatever the case, idols will pull us away from our Heavenly Father, and they will never truly fulfill us. They tempt us to meet our needs apart from God. Idols cause fear and worry because, through them, we place our hope in something besides God alone. The weeds of idols choke out the fruit God wants to grow in our lives.

In the book of Daniel, we see how God's children responded when they were commanded to worship idols. In Daniel chapter 2, we find that Shadrach, Meshach, and Abednego were Hebrew captives taken to Babylon under King Nebuchadnezzar. There they were trained to work for the king, who placed them in high positions over the administration in Babylon. They had status, they had favor, they had everything they needed, and more. Shadrach, Meshach, and Abednego grew up learning and knowing God's law. They knew that Deuteronomy 6:5 commanded them to love the Lord their God with all their hearts. They knew from Exodus 20:3–5 that they should have no other gods and not make any idols. Even being captured as slaves and serving the king, they knew what God required of them. In Daniel chapter 3, we see their faith put to the test. Everyone in Babylon was commanded to bow down and worship the golden image. Those who refused would be put to death. These three Hebrew slaves who had favor with the king faced a tough choice. To bow down meant to save their lives. Not to bow down meant death in a blazing furnace.

I love their response!

"If it be so, our God whom we serve is able

to deliver us from the furnace of blazing fire;

and He will deliver us out of your hand, O king.

But even if He does not, let it be known to you, O king,

that we are not going to serve your gods

or worship the golden image that you have set up."

—Daniel 3:17–18

These three knew God's Law, and they purposed in their hearts to obey—no matter the cost. There may be idols in our lives that are keeping us from wholeheartedly loving and serving the Lord. This week we'll learn to recognize the idols that bring us fear and worry. We need to destroy them for the seed of faith to grow!

## DAY 1

God alone is to be worshiped. While we know this in our heads, sometimes our hearts can have little gods or idols that clamor for our attention. We allow those idols to take God's place. When we trust in something other than God, those idols can grow the weed of fear.

Write out this week's memory verse, Deuteronomy 6:5.

_____

_____

Define what an idol is.

_____

_____

Often when we think of idols, we think of the golden calf that the Israelites worshiped. That was a pretty obvious idol. Some of our idols might be obvious, but many disguise themselves. List examples of modern-day idols.

_____

_____

_____

Exodus 20:3–6 gives us the first two commandments. What are they?

_____

_____

God is quite serious about our devotion. When you love the Lord with every part of your being, there is no room for idols! Spend time in prayer asking the Lord to fill you with love for Him—and Him alone. Ask the Holy Spirit to show you this week where there might be idols in your life.

# DAY 2

God hates idols. Whenever God gave new territory to the Israelites, He reminded them to destroy all the idols. When they obeyed, they experienced blessings. When they disobeyed, they experienced a lot of pain. This week we'll focus on destroying idols. Pray and ask the Holy Spirit to teach you as you read Deuteronomy 4:1–24. Write down your observations—what stood out to you?

Looking at your list of fears and worries, could any of those fears be idolatry? Are you seeking satisfaction from a source that can't truly satisfy?

Indulging in idolatry leads us to believe that we need more than what God provides. Do you trust the Lord to provide you with exactly what you need?

We destroy the idols by confessing them as sin to the Lord. As we destroy the weeds of idols, more room is available for the seed of faith to grow. Spend time confessing any idols the Lord reveals to you.

Pray and ask the Holy Spirit to teach you as you read and meditate on Psalm 23.

What does David declare in verse 1?

_____

_____

What does a shepherd do?

_____

_____

What does the Shepherd do for us in verses 2–3?

_____

_____

The Lord is with us in pleasant times (verses 2–3) and difficult times (verses 4–5). Why does David not fear according to verse 4?

_____

_____

A little secret in overcoming our fears is to learn that His presence in our lives is enough. What are the promises in verse 6?

_____

_____

Make this psalm your prayer to the Lord.

## DAY 3

Pray and invite the Holy Spirit to teach you as you read and meditate on Psalm 115.

What is verse 1 saying?

_____

_____

_____

Verse 2 tells us that other nations were questioning where the Israelites' God was during their troubles. Do you ever feel that way?

_____

_____

What is the answer in verse 3?

_____

_____

God is sovereign over everything, and He promises never to leave us. Reading verses 4–8, what do you discover about idols?

_____

_____

Idols are foolish and powerless. They cannot help us. Our flesh, the world, and the enemy will tell us that we need more. There is a command for us repeated in verses 9–11. What is it?

_____

_____

We choose to trust in the Lord despite our challenges. What will happen when we trust Him (verses 12–14)?

_____

_____

_____

Spend time praying and asking the Lord to reveal any idols that might be in your life. Confess those idols and declare your desire to trust in Him alone.

# DAY 4

Money can be an idol. Whether you need more or have more than enough, it can become a god when we focus too much on it. Ask the Holy Spirit to help you understand as you read Matthew 6:19–24.

What does Jesus tell us to avoid? Why?

_____

_____

What should we do instead?

_____

_____

What do we learn in verse 24?

_____

_____

Read Hebrews 13:5–6.

What do we need to do?

_____

_____

Whether we have little or abundance, we are called to be content with what we have. What did Jesus promise us in verse 5?

_____

_____

Riches may come and go, but our security is in Christ alone; so that we may confidently say *what*, according to verse 6?

_____

_____

Let's go back to Matthew 6 and finish reading 25–34. Interestingly, Jesus talks about money, then immediately discusses anxiety. Summarize His message in these passages.

_____

_____

_____

_____

Write out verse 33, underline the command and double underline the promise.

_____

_____

_____

Don't worry! God will provide exactly what you need for this day. Do you believe Him? Spend time in prayer thanking Him that He will provide. Commit to Him your desire not to worry.

## DAY 5

Paul's letter to Timothy encouraged him to fight the good fight. Pray and ask the Holy Spirit to teach you as you read 1 Timothy 6:6–18.

What strikes you in verses 6–10?

_____

_____

_____

What can happen if we let love of money—our want for money—become our focus instead of God?

_____

_____

_____

What are we to do in verses 11–12?

_____

_____

_____

There are instructions for those who have plenty. What are we instructed to do in verses 17–18?

_____

_____

_____

Placing something higher than God in our lives is idolatry. There is no other besides the great I AM. Only the true God can save us.

Write out Acts 4:12.

_____

_____

_____

_____

_____

Let Jesus alone sit on the throne of your life. Spend time in prayer thanking the Lord that there is no other God like Him and that He alone is able to save you and meet your needs.

# KNOW WHO YOU ARE

**WEEK 6**

For roots to spread out and be healthy, the soil needs to be loose. Preparing the soil of our hearts requires us to look up and know who God is. It also requires us to know who we are in Christ. Many fears stem from how we view ourselves and how we think others view us. Our insecurities can rear up, leaving us stuck in fear. When you form your identity from anything besides what God has declared you to be, you are left with feelings of failure, fears, and worries. When you are unsure of your identity, that soil in your heart gets packed so tightly that it stifles the roots.

Our identity does not come from what people, the world, the mirror, or the scale says about us! We are not identified by our successes or our failures. Amen! If we don't know who we really are, then our flesh, the world, and the enemy will toss us in every direction. The weed of fear will continue to grow and cause us to doubt—to worry that we are not enough. It will be exhausting, discouraging, and defeating.

So, who are you *really*? In Christ you are identified by what God declares about you. In Him is where we find our worth and approval.

> But now, thus says the Lord, your Creator, O Jacob,
>
> And He who formed you, O Israel,
>
> "Do not fear, for I have redeemed you;
>
> I have called you by name; you are Mine!
>
> —Isaiah 43:1

God has called us by name, He has redeemed us, and we are His! This week we will look at what God says about us. Sometimes we don't feel as if what God says about us could possibly be true. However, our feelings don't change what God has declared to be true. We choose by faith to believe what God says is true, and then our feelings will catch up! In His Word, God tells us that we are His workmanship, His masterpiece (Ephesians 2:10). Maybe you are not feeling like a masterpiece today, but the truth is that God has declared this over you; and that's how He sees you. You are a masterpiece in the making; He isn't finished with any of us yet!

I went amethyst mining once. It was quite an adventure. Not only did I find some beautiful jewels, but the Lord taught me many lessons. On the outside, amethysts appear dirty and not very exciting. When you gently chip away the exterior and uncover some of the dirt and grime, you discover the beautiful gems inside. Psalm 139:1 tells us that God has searched us and knows us. When God searches us, He sees the jewel underneath! My prayer for you this week is that God will open your eyes to see past the dirt and grime to all that He has made you to be.

If we believe that we aren't enough, that we are failures, or that we are too fearful, then that is how we will behave. We're called to walk in a manner worthy of our calling. When we believe what God says about us, we behave differently. If our identity is wrapped up in our appearance, our talent, our career, or our things . . . we're in trouble. Beauty is fleeting, wrinkles will come, someone more talented than we are will take over . . . but if we know who we are in Christ, we never need to fear those changes. God has given you a new identity; let it define who you are!

## DAY 1

Our desire to be accepted by others can cause fear. Our doubts can overwhelm us. Will I measure up? Will I be good enough? Will others accept me? If we let anything but our Lord define who we are, we will always fall short. This is a frustrating place to be! When we place our faith in Jesus, we are born again—given a brand-new start. At that moment, we are given a new identity.

Write out this week's memory verse, 2 Corinthians 5:17.

_____

_____

_____

_____

What does it mean that you are a new creation?

_____

_____

_____

What does this look like in your life?

At the moment of your salvation, you were put on a new path, given a new start. You are no longer known by your old self, now you are known by your new identity. Looking through your list of fears and worries, are any related to how you think people view you? It takes time to learn to live in our new position in Christ. This week, pray and ask the Lord to show you who you are in Christ.

# DAY 2

Maybe it's been a long time since you first placed your faith in Jesus, or maybe it was not too long ago. Or maybe you have not yet made the decision to follow Christ. No matter where you are, it's good to remember why we need Jesus.

The foundation for our hope in moving from fear to faith is based on a personal relationship with Jesus Christ. Write out the following verses that explain why it is that we need a Savior. Pray and ask the Holy Spirit to speak to your heart.

Romans 3:23

_____

_____

_____

Romans 6:23

_____

_____

_____

Romans 5:8

_____

_____

_____

Romans 10:9–11

_____

_____

_____

1 John 5:11–13

_____

_____

If this is all new to you, spend time with the Lord thanking Him that He has provided a way for you to know Him. Acknowledge your sins, ask God for forgiveness, and place your trust in Christ. When you do so, eternal life begins, and the Holy Spirit will enable you to conquer fear and worry. If trusting in Christ has been your life for a while, it never gets old! Thank Him that you belong to Him!

## DAY 3

Pray and ask the Holy Spirit to teach you as you read and meditate on Psalm 139.

What does the Lord know about you? How involved is He in your life? Write down at least ten answers to these questions.

_____

_____

_____

_____

_____

_____

_____

In your present situation—in your worries and fears—can you trust that the Lord knows you better than you know yourself . . . and that He has a plan for you?

What do verses 1–3 tell us?

_____

_____

_____

_____

Sometimes our struggles can drag on over years, even decades; and we can believe that God doesn't see us—and that He doesn't care. This is not true! He sees every part of us and our lives—He hasn't missed a detail because He cares for us.

Verse 1 tells us that the Lord has already searched our hearts. He knows what is there. In verse 23, David gave the Lord permission to search his heart. Do you know what this means? It is surrendering to the Lord. Sometimes in our fears and worries, we become angry at God because He hasn't helped us in the way that we thought He should—or when we thought He should. We need to surrender our anger to the Lord by confessing. Pray Psalm 139:23–24 to Him and let Him show you if any of your fears and worries are simply wrong thinking based on trying to get approval from the world. Then confess these things to the Lord and thank Him that you are a new creation approved by Him!

## DAY 4

Make a list of the things the world says we should be.

_____

_____

_____

_____

_____

Next, mark any items in your list above that you have believed. Stop letting the world set the agenda for who you need to be—instead let God declare who you are. Confess to the Lord the areas where you have let the world tell you your worth.

Write out your testimony of when you recognized your need for a Savior and how the Lord Jesus changed you.

_____

_____

_____

_____

_____

As you read 1 Peter 2:9–10, ask God to impress upon your heart, your wonderful new identity. According to these verses, what does God declare you to be in Christ?

_____

_____

_____

What are we to do with this new position we have?

_____

_____

_____

_____

Spend time thanking the Lord for calling you out of darkness and giving you a new identity.

## DAY 5

Knowing our identity in Christ takes time to learn and we must choose by faith to believe that what God says about us is true. The New Testament is filled with Scriptures that tell us what God has declared us to be. As you come across them in your readings, meditate on them. They will change your perspective!

Write out 2 Timothy 1:7.

What has God not given us?

A spirit of fear is not from the Lord. That was part of our old self and our old way of life, but in Christ we are no longer known that way! In Christ we have all hope that God is bigger than anything we are facing—and faithful to help us walk through whatever He asks us to.

According to this verse, what spirit has the Lord given us?

As we learn to walk in our new identity in Christ, we need to stop seeing ourselves as the old person. We also need to stop labeling our brothers and sisters in Christ with their old identities. Read 2 Corinthians 5:16–21.

Why do we no longer need to identify with the old self?

In Christ we are connected to the great I AM, and we have everything we long for. Many of our fears and worries stem from how we think others view us. When we know that we are fully accepted by God, we will stop striving for the approval of others.

With our new identity we have purpose. Some fears might be rooted in our need to have purpose. What purposes are we called to fulfill now that we are in Christ?

Read John 1:12–13.

When we receive God's gift of Jesus, what do we become?

Read Romans 8:31–39. What are these passages saying?

Some of our fears and worries might be rooted in our need for security. No matter what goes on around us, in Christ we are secure! Nothing can separate us from the love of God!

Spend time with the Lord asking Him to teach you who you are in Christ, and choose by faith to believe what He has declared about you through His Word.

# THANK HIM

### WEEK 7

Did you know that you can determine how healthy a plant is by the health of the root system? We're getting healthy roots to nourish our faith! Worship is one discipline that will grow our faith. A thankful heart is another way to nourish that plant. Did you know that you get to *choose* to have a thankful heart?

Do you know of any ungrateful children? Does it frustrate you that they don't seem to appreciate all that they have and everything that's done for them? Does this attitude make you want to pour out your blessings on them? Do you love them less because they're ungrateful?

These are all good questions to ponder. God has children like this as well! He does not love them less, but I do believe that they miss out on many of His blessings. An unthankful heart chooses to look at the negative rather than focusing on the positive. When we choose thankfulness, we're tearing down strongholds of grumbling, complaining, bitterness, and envy. A thankful heart will change our perspective.

> I shall remember the deeds of the Lord;
> Surely I will remember Your wonders of old.
> I will meditate on all Your work
> And muse on Your deeds.
> Your way, O God, is holy;
> What god is great like our God?
> —Psalm 77:11–13

Worrying is a digression, it takes our eyes off Jesus and leads us down the wrong path. When we remember what the Lord has done, it lifts our gaze back up to Him and puts us back on the right path. In this passage we're called to meditate on what the Lord has done. When was the last time you reflected on what God has done for you? When we look back at all that He has done, our hearts are encouraged. It strengthens our faith, and then we can look forward to the future with faith and hope. Everything that God does, He does with purpose. When I remember His deeds, I look back and see that He was working things out for His purposes and His plans. It's important that you remember all God has done for you. It's important to have a thankful heart!

## DAY 1

Looking back and thanking God for what He has done will help us look to the future with faith.

Write out and memorize 1 Thessalonians 5:16–18.

_____

_____

_____

When are we to rejoice?

_____

_____

_____

How often should we pray?

_____

_____

_____

This doesn't mean we talk to God nonstop. It means we are to persevere in praying consistently—exactly what we've been doing each day of our study!

In what are we to give thanks?

_____

_____

_____

It is easy to give thanks when the way is pleasant and smooth. It is an act of obedience to give thanks when we are pressed and challenged. God is over everything that we go through, and He makes us more like Christ in the process; this should bring us a spirit of thankfulness.

For what are you thankful today?

_____

_____

_____

Spend time rejoicing, praying, and giving thanks!

## DAY 2

The Word of God is filled with verses on giving thanks to the Lord. Pray and ask the Holy Spirit to teach you as you read the following verses. Summarize what each one tells us about thankfulness.

Ephesians 5:3–4

_____

_____

Ephesians 5:20

_____

_____

Colossians 3:15–17

_____

_____

Colossians 4:2

_____

_____

Sometimes it's difficult to be thankful amidst our struggles and fears, but it's all a matter of perspective. Read the following verses and write down what you can be thankful for.

Romans 8:28

_____

_____

1 Corinthians 10:13

Philippians 4:19

1 Peter 5:7–10

For what are you thankful today? Rejoice, pray, and give thanks to Him.

## DAY 3

When we choose to remember and thank the Lord for what He has done, our faith will grow.

Joshua was the man who the Lord appointed to lead the Israelites into the Promised Land. After 40 years of wandering in the wilderness, they were finally going to enter. However, the Jordan River was in flood stage. Joshua chapter 3 outlines how the Lord got two million people across the flooded Jordan in one day. Pray and ask the Holy Spirit to teach you as you read Joshua chapter 4.

What did God tell Joshua to do in verses 2–3?

_____

_____

What was the purpose of this in verses 6–7?

_____

_____

Remembering is important! In verses 20–23 what did Joshua tell the people to do?

Faith grows when we remember what the Lord has done for us and then tell our stories to our children, grandchildren, neighbors, and anyone who will listen. According to verse 24, what will we know when we pass along the stories of God's faithfulness?

_____

_____

_____

For what are you thankful today? Rejoice, pray, and thank Him.

## DAY 4

Passover was the feast that the Israelites celebrated to remember the Lord leading them out of Egypt. Pray and ask the Holy Spirit to teach you as you read and meditate on Psalm 136, which was recited at the Passover.

What is the command in verses 1–3?

_____

_____

Why should we do this?

_____

_____

Define *everlasting lovingkindness.*

_____

_____

List as many things as you can for which the Israelites were thankful.

_____

_____

_____

For what are you thankful today? Rejoice, pray, and thank Him.

_____

_____

_____

# DAY 5

Today we'll examine what Jesus had to say about remembering. Pray and ask the Holy Spirit to guide and teach you as you read Luke 22:7–19.

What feast were they celebrating?

_____

_____

_____

They were remembering and thanking God for what He had done. Remembering and thanking God should become a habit in our lives.

What does Jesus say in verses 16 and 18?

_____

_____

_____

When we celebrate communion, we are remembering that He is coming back!

What are we instructed to do in verse 19?

_____

_____

_____

We still celebrate communion to remember what Christ did when He died for us on the cross. We remember that His death covered our sins and that now we are united with Him.

Read 1 Corinthians 11:28. What are we reminded to do?

_____

_____

_____

When we do this, we remember that we still need Jesus every day, and we cannot make it on our own without Him.

For what are you thankful today? Rejoice, pray, and thank Him.

# PRAY

**WEEK 8**

For a plant to bear fruit, it must be exposed to the sun. Sunshine supplies the plant with energy. For us to bear fruit for the Lord, we must spend time with the Son. Time spent with Jesus will energize and strengthen us!

> I am the vine, you are the branches;
>
> he who abides in Me and I in him, he bears much fruit,
>
> for apart from Me you can do nothing.
>
> —John 15:5

To abide in Christ is to stay close in our relationship with Him. We do this by obeying His commands. As a parent, when I give an instruction to my child, I have an expectation that obedience will follow. When obedience isn't the response, our relationship is disrupted. When we obey the Lord, we are keeping our relationship with Him united. In growing our faith, it is vitally important that we abide in Him, and it is our choice to do it. When we abide we are connected to the vine and we do everything with Him. If we abide in Christ, the promise is we will bear much fruit. It does not say if we work harder, try harder or attend more Bible studies. It is our abiding in Him that produces much fruit. When we abide in Him, He will fill our garden with fruit—and lots of it! As we go from fear to faith, He is making us more like Him. We will bear the fruit of the Spirit—love, joy, peace, patience, kindness, goodness, gentleness and self- control. Life is a lot more pleasant when we have this growing in us rather than the weeds that produce hate, anger, chaos, impatience, unkindness, harshness and unrestraint. There will also be fruit that will grow as we pour into other's lives. Every area of our lives is an opportunity to bear fruit.

Praying is one way to stay close to Christ. Prayer is declaring our dependence on Him because apart from Him, we can do nothing. Prayer changes everything. It changes your perspective on your problems. When we go to the Lord with our fears and worries rather than trying to handle them on our own, we are changed. Prayer is talking with God; it's a relationship with Him. Have you ever had any friends who only seem to talk about themselves? This is exhausting. We all want to be heard. A healthy relationship never has a one-sided conversation. Prayer is not simply bringing our lists of wants or desires to the Lord with the expectation that He will give us everything we want. Prayer is our way to converse with God and listen to Him through His Word and His Spirit.

## DAY 1

As we continue to grow that seed of faith, our prayer life will need to grow as well. In prayer we are connected to the One who is all powerful, all knowing, and always with us. My goodness! Why wouldn't we want to spend time talking with and listening to Him?

Write out our memory verse, 2 Chronicles 7:14.

_____

_____

_____

_____

_____

God commanded us to do several things in this verse; list them.

_____

_____

_____

_____

What does God promise to do IF we have done our part?

_____

_____

_____

_____

Write out Philippians 4:6–7. Underline the command and double underline the promise.

_____

_____

_____

_____

_____

In this verse, Paul tells us to pray instead of worrying. Prayer is where we meet God, gain His perspective, and receive His power to walk through the storms of life. Spend time in prayer with your list of fears and worries, asking the Holy Spirit to show you His perspective and strengthen your faith.

## DAY 2

Prayer is a dialogue with the Most High. Read through the following verses and write down what you learn. Pray and ask the Holy Spirit for help!

Psalm 5:3

_____

_____

Psalm 34:15

_____

_____

Psalm 66:18

_____

_____

Psalm 145:18

_____

_____

_____

James 4:3

_____

_____

_____

James 5:13–16

1 John 5:14

Isn't it amazing that the great I AM is interested in listening to us? Read Psalm 55:22. What are we instructed to do?

What does it mean to cast our cares or burdens?

What is His promise when we do this?

Meditating on the verses above, spend time in prayer casting your cares, fears, and worries to Him.

# DAY 3

The Psalms are powerful prayers of worship, confession, requests, and thankfulness. Today we will spend time praying the Psalms. It's easy, sweet, and powerful!

Read and meditate through Psalm 1.

Who is blessed according to verse 1?

_____

_____

_____

In verse 2, why is the person blessed?

_____

_____

_____

What promises will be received in verse 3?

_____

_____

_____

Have you ever wondered what it means to prosper, according to the Scriptures? It means to be spiritually healthy and fruitful. It is important to understand what we are praying, or we might think that God is not answering us!

What happens to the wicked, according to verses 4–6?

_____

_____

_____

Make this psalm your prayer to the Lord. Pray aloud to help you concentrate and avoid distractions. Make it personal.

Whenever you pray His Word, you are proclaiming God's promises back to Him. His promises will always be fulfilled.

When we have fears or worries, we find our hope and instruction in the Word. Spend time praying through your favorite psalms or some that we've read in this study: Psalm 23, 27, 34, 56, 115, 121, 136, and 139.

# DAY 4

We'll spend the next two days looking at what Jesus said about prayer. Pray and ask the Holy Spirit to help you understand as you read Matthew 6:7–15.

According to verse 7, how are we not to pray?

_____

_____

What does our heavenly Father know in verse 8?

_____

_____

Why, then, do you think we pray?

_____

_____

_____

God knows our needs, but He desires our hearts. Just like we love to spend time and be in relationship with our dearest friends, God desires that time with us even more. So, we spend time with Him conversing in prayer. It isn't a one-way conversation. It requires us to be quiet and listen to Him through His Word and His Spirit.

Verses 9–14 are known as the Lord's Prayer. It is a model for prayer.

Prayer isn't about a list that we take to God for Him to fill. What is an important element of prayer, according to verse 9?

_____

_____

What is an important element according to verse 10?

How are you doing in surrendering to His will in your prayers? This requires us to closely examine our hearts when we take our requests to Him. Are you able to say in the storms and worries of life, "Your will be done, not mine"? How about "Your timing, Lord, not mine"?

What does verse 11 say?

Did you notice the words *this day*? These words lead me to believe we should go to Him in prayer *every* day! Spend time in prayer with Him, incorporating some of the elements of prayer we have looked at today.

# DAY 5

Pray and ask the Holy Spirit to help you as we finish off our study of Matthew 6:7–15. Review these passages.

Write out verse 12. What is the request we make of God? What are we expected to do?

_____

_____

_____

_____

If confession is not yet a daily part of your prayer time, be sure to add it. To grow in our relationship with the Lord, we need to be quick to confess and quick to forgive others. We must be obedient to His commands if we want to experience His promises!

What does verse 13 tell us?

_____

_____

What do we learn from verses 14–15, which follow the Lord's Prayer?

_____

_____

How important is it that we forgive others? Why?

_____

_____

Read John 10:27-29. What does it say?

_____

_____

_____

_____

We cannot lose our salvation. Romans 8:38–39 promises us that we cannot be separated from Christ. When we don't forgive, our salvation is not at risk; but our relationship with the Lord will be strained because we are disobeying Him. Behind some of our fears and worries could be bitterness that we have not properly handled. When we are not abiding in Christ and obeying His commands, we will feel anxious. This anxiety, in reality, is a gift—a warning from the Holy Spirit that something is not right. Spend time with the Lord and ask Him if you need to forgive anyone. Choose to forgive; the Lord will bring healing to your heart and mind!

# THWART THE LIES

## WEEK 9

There are lies behind our fears and worries. The enemy tries to deceive us that God is not who He says He is, that He will not do what He promises, and that we are not enough in Christ. These lies are simply more weeds to be pulled out. Did you know that the mustard plant releases compounds to keep pests away? Our plant of faith will also drive the enemy away!

> Now the serpent was more crafty than any beast of the field which the Lord God had made. And he said to the woman, "Indeed, has God said, 'You shall not eat from any tree of the garden'?"
> —Genesis 3:1

The serpent was crafty. He was deceitful. Lies are tricky; they almost sound like truth. When I planted my yard with wildflowers, many weeds were able to grow because I couldn't tell which was a flower and which was a weed. Even Satan disguises himself as an angel of light (2 Corinthians 11:14). If he came to us as in the old cartoons with a red suit and horns, speaking horrible things to us about God, we would recognize—and dismiss—him right away. However, he comes disguised as angel of light; he is crafty and subtle. Satan's tactic is to lie. If we believe his lies, he has us right where he wants us—discouraged, despairing, and defeated.

"Has God said?" This was the question that Satan posed to Eve in the garden. The question implied that God was not good or fair because they were not allowed to eat from every tree. Satan wants us to doubt God's character. He wants us to believe that God is holding out on us. He will try to get us to believe the lie that God really doesn't care. If God really loved me, I wouldn't have to go through this—this is the lie. Going through challenges and storms is one way that He molds us into the image of Christ.

Satan loves confusion. Notice that in the passage he said, "from any tree." He wants us to doubt God's Word. When we doubt God, we act independently of Him, which is sin because we are placing our own will above God's. Eve believed the lies of Satan, and then both she and Adam disobeyed God's words to them, placing their will above His. It all started with deception.

The battle always begins in the mind—the battle to believe the truth or the lie. When we choose to renew our minds and believe the truth of God's Word, we will experience freedom. In the same way that we pull out the weeds of unbelief and idols, we need to thwart the lies. Let's prevent Satan from gaining ground in our lives by removing the weeds of lies that we have allowed to grow in our hearts. As the Lord exposes lies that you have believed, renounce them; then replace them with what God says is true. Declaring truth is a powerful weapon!

## DAY 1

Usually there are lies behind our fears—lies about God, His promises, our identity. Satan is the father of lies, as we see in John 8:44. If we believe his lies, he has us right where he wants us—afraid, discouraged, and defeated. Do you know what truth does? It sets us free! It will bring us to faith, hope, and victory!

Pray and ask the Holy Spirit to guard your mind as you read these Scriptures.

Read John 14:6. Who is Jesus according to this passage?

_____

_____

Read John 17:17. What does Jesus pray that the Lord will do with His Word?

_____

_____

Our memory verse this week is John 8:32. Write it below.

_____

_____

_____

_____

The only way to thwart the lies is to stand in truth. Jesus is the truth; and God will sanctify us in the Word, which is truth. Spend time in prayer with your list of fears and worries, and ask the Holy Spirit to show you the lies you've believed about each fear or worry. Remember, the lies will be about God's character, His promises, or your position in Christ. This might be challenging, but as you go through the week, the Holy Spirit will teach you how to recognize the lies.

# DAY 2

Have you always been a worrier? Did you have family members who were worriers? Do you believe this is how God created you—and that you'll always be this way?

_____

_____

_____

_____

_____

Remember—you have been given a new identity. *Worrier* is not part of that identity. You might have had generations before you who struggled with worrying, but in Christ we get to break those bonds. We don't need to take them on as our own. We are not destined to be worriers, but faith-filled warriors! By faith we choose to believe that what God says about us is true. It takes time and practice to learn to walk in the new self. Do not get discouraged.

Our fears have an object—something or someone that seems to have power over us. The well-known acronym for FEAR is False Evidence Appearing Real. Nothing is greater than God's power. The enemy wants us to believe that whatever we fear is more powerful than God . . . but the truth is, God is greater.

Our worries are different from fears. Worries are the *what ifs* in life. Worries are exhausting. They can consume us and keep us awake at night. The *what ifs* are the situations that are not happening right now—except in our minds. Have you ever noticed your mind going to the worst-case scenario? Go through your list of fears and worries to identify which ones are worries instead of fears. Spend time in prayer declaring that God is always with you, all knowing and all powerful in each fear and worry.

## DAY 3

What do we do with our fears and worries once we can identify the lies behind them? We renounce the lies and replace them with truth. Remember—it is the truth that sets us free! We declare out loud to God that we reject the lies we have believed, and at the same time we give notice to Satan that we choose truth instead. When we expose the lie and reject it, we pull out another weed of fear.

After we have renounced the lie, we need to replace it with truth. This requires us to know truth. It's a process, and the Holy Spirit is faithful to help us. Spend time in prayer with the Lord with your list of fears and worries. For each one say, "I renounce the fear of _____ and the lie that _____." Then declare what is true: "The truth is, God _____."

Let's start with an example. If layoffs are taking place at my company and I am fearful of losing my job, my prayer might go like this: "I renounce the fear of **losing my job** and the lie that **my needs won't be met**. The truth is, God, you will supply all my needs, **Philippians 4:19**."

This is hard work! But when we pull out those weeds of lies, fruit will grow!

## DAY 4

When we are anxious and worried, we create worst-case scenarios in our minds. Our lives rarely play out to the worst case, but we sure do waste a lot of our time and energy being consumed by it. When you learn to renew your mind and choose to believe the truth of His Word, you experience freedom.

Worrying is being double-minded. Read James 1:5–8. What is James saying in these verses?

_____

_____

_____

When we worry, we go back and forth from belief to unbelief. We are tossed around like the waves—a very unpleasant ride. Spend time confessing your worry—your doublemindedness to the Lord.

Read 2 Corinthians 10:3–5.

Fear and worry are in the flesh, but we can't battle them in the flesh. It's not possible just to try harder to overcome fear. We need help!

What do you notice about the weapons we are to use in this battle, according to verse 4?

_____

_____

Fear and worry are fortresses that need to be destroyed. We can do this only with divine power.

God tells us to take every thought captive to the obedience of Christ. We have power to control the _what if_ thoughts that can paralyze us, but we must play our part!

Read Romans 12:2. What are we not to do?

_____

_____

In what ways have you been conformed to this world?

_____

_____

Spend time in prayer, confessing this to the Lord.

According to the verse, how will we be transformed?

_____

_____

Renewing our minds is how we break the strongholds of fear and worry. Remember, we have the power to control our minds!

Sometimes we forget that we can choose our thoughts. When those little nagging thoughts pop into your head, do not let them simmer! Renounce the lies out loud and replace them with God's truth.

Remember—it's a process! Don't get discouraged.

What do you put in your mind? What you read and watch will influence the way you think. Do your reading and viewing habits glorify God? We need to guard our minds; we are called to be holy and set apart from the world. When we are not living a life set apart for Him, we'll feel anxious. Remember, this is a gift from the Spirit reminding us to turn back to Him.

Spend time with the Lord right now and ask Him to begin renewing your mind, improving how you respond to all the *what ifs* of life.

## DAY 5

Pray and ask the Holy Spirit to teach you as you read and meditate on Psalm 91. This is a psalm of trust that can help us contemplate the *what ifs* and then inspire us to stand on truth.

What are the four names of God shown in verses 1–2? Write down the meaning of each name.

_____

_____

_____

_____

In these verses, you'll also find four words that describe Him. List them and write down the definition of each.

_____

_____

_____

_____

In verse 3, we see that He will deliver you. What does this mean?

_____

_____

Describe verse 4.

_____

_____

What will you not fear in verses 5–8?

_____

_____

_____

If any *what ifs* have you worried, God has you covered. You can choose to believe His Word and apply it to your circumstances.

Write out verses 14–15. Underline the command and double underline His promise.

_____

_____

_____

Love Him and call upon Him. He will set you securely on high! Now spend some time praying through this psalm. Make it personal. It will bless you!

# KNOW HIS WORD

## WEEK 10

Throughout our study we've looked at who God is and who we are in Christ; and this week we'll look at His promises. As we learn and grow in these areas, we are keeping the soil of our garden loose and soft. The more time we spend in His Word and receive it, the more our roots will grow deep and strong. Knowing His Word will guard our hearts and minds . . . and keep the weeds from growing back. His Word will always put us on the right path.

Have you ever gone exploring? A map is a very helpful tool, whether you're out in the wilderness or navigating city streets. I love my map app! It tells me exactly where to go, when to turn, and my estimated arrival time. When I make a mistake, it doesn't yell at me; it just reroutes me! As we navigate from fear to faith, God's Word is our map. Scripture helps us gain God's perspective. It tells us exactly what to do—and when we make a mistake it will reroute us! Another useful tool when exploring is a compass. It helps determine our directions and always points due north. It's up to us to follow. Philippians 4:8 is like a compass for our thoughts. When we're tempted to fear and worry, we can line up our thoughts with this verse—and it will point us back in the right direction.

> Finally, brethren, whatever is true, whatever is honorable, whatever is right, whatever is pure, whatever is lovely, whatever is of good repute, if there is any excellence and if anything worthy of praise, dwell on these things.
> —Philippians 4:8

Last week we looked at Satan's tactic of trying to fill our thoughts with lies. The only way to break from his lies is to know the truth. The Word has all we need. It will guide us and navigate us through any wilderness—any storm. Our job is to be students of the Word. The Bible won't help us if we leave it on a shelf, unopened. It won't help us if we don't study it to understand, and it won't help us if we don't actually apply it to our lives! This takes training. We need to diligently spend time in the Word, to strengthen our faith. Remember, we have the ability and responsibility to control our own thoughts. When we take our thoughts captive and line them up with the truth of God's Word, our fears disappear! With God's Word as our map, we'll be able to safely navigate storms that come our way. This is walking by faith—not fear!

## DAY 1

The more we know the Word of God, the more we recognize those sneaky lies from the enemy. This happens when we renew our minds in the Word.

Write out our memory verse, Psalm 119:165.

_____

_____

_____

_____

Who are the ones who love His law?

_____

_____

We can say that we love the Word, but if we don't obey it, we deceive ourselves. This produces anxiety.

According to the verse, what happens to those who love and obey His law?

_____

_____

When the temptations and storms of life hit, these people will not fall away. They will have His perfect peace in the midst of it all because they are abiding in Him. Read the following verses and write down what we can do instead of turning to fear.

Ephesians 4:20–24

_____

_____

Colossians 3:1–2

1 Peter 1:13–16

This week spend time in prayer thanking God for His Word and asking Him to renew your mind with His Truth.

## DAY 2

Pray and ask the Holy Spirit to guide you as you read and meditate on Psalm 19.

What do verses 1–6 describe?

_____

_____

_____

Verses 7–8 have to do with God's Word. What do we gain from the Word, according to these verses?

_____

_____

_____

In verse 9, how is the fear of the Lord described?

_____

_____

_____

How are the judgments of the Lord described?

_____

_____

What do we learn from verses 10–11?

_____

_____

What is the meaning of verse 14?

_____

_____

_____

Now spend time praying through this psalm, making it personal. Thank the Lord for the power of His Word and declare to Him your desire to renew your mind in it.

# DAY 3

Knowing God's Word gives us direction for our lives. We often wonder, what God's will is for our lives. Studying, meditating, and applying His Word will keep us in His will. Psalm 119 is the longest psalm and the longest chapter in the Bible. This entire psalm is about the Word of God and how it contains everything we need to know.

When you're looking for direction, need encouragement, struggling with fear, looking for wisdom, wanting to know how to live in obedience, learning how to serve the Lord . . . read the Word. It has all the answers!

We'll spend the next two days studying Psalm 119. Pray and ask the Holy Spirit to help you as you read through the entire psalm today. Do not be afraid or overwhelmed by the length!

After you read through the psalm, write down a few observations that struck you during your first reading.

Read through it again and write down as many synonyms for the Word of God that you can find.

Spend time in prayer with this psalm, asking God to give you a hunger and thirst for His Word.

## DAY 4

Begin your time today by inviting the Holy Spirit to impress upon your heart the truths of Psalm 119. Read through the psalm again, this time noticing all the emotions the psalmist is experiencing. This psalm is all about the joy and pain each one of us experiences. Write down the emotions you find as you read. Can you relate to any of them?

_____

_____

_____

_____

This psalm is divided into stanzas; each is a prayer that the psalmist brings before the Lord. These prayers are not fancy—they're straight from the heart. This is exactly how we should go to the Lord! He's not impressed with our choice of words. We can't fool Him; He already sees what's in our hearts. He simply wants us to go to Him and trust Him.

The psalmist believes God's Word is true. What he continually prays is that God would make His Word real in his life. I love this! He's asking God to work His Word out in him—renewing the mind.

How real is God's Word to you?

_____

_____

_____

On our journey from fear to faith, we've been asking God to make His Word real in us so we can walk by faith. This is important to learn because we'll be doing it for the rest of our days on earth!

Maybe, as you read through this psalm, you really relate to certain stanzas. Spend time praying through the verses that are your heart's cry to the Lord; make it your own request to Him. Pray and ask the Holy Spirit to make His Word real in you.

# DAY 5

Jesus knew, studied, and memorized Scripture. He is our example. Pray and ask the Holy Spirit to help you as you read Matthew 4:1–11.

Who led Jesus into the wilderness?

_____

_____

What do we notice in verse 2?

_____

_____

Who came to Him in verse 3?

_____

_____

Every time Satan tempted Him, how did Jesus respond?

_____

_____

When we are pelted with the lies of the enemy, we need to respond with the Word of God. When we are tempted to look at our circumstances and worry, what promise do we have in 1 Corinthians 10:13?

_____

_____

_____

The temptation is to freak out and worry when the storms of life come, but we can choose to trust God in times when it's scary and we're unsure of the outcome.

Write out Proverbs 30:5. Underline the command and double underline God's promise.

---

---

---

Spend time in prayer, thanking Him for His Word, which is true. With your list of fears, choose to take refuge in Him. He will be your shield!

# STAND FIRM

## WEEK 11

A plant's roots have two roles. One is to take up water and nutrients from the soil, and the other is to anchor it into the ground. Our little seed of faith grows deep roots and keeps us anchored in Him. Storms, fears, and worries will come; but when we're rooted in Him, we stand firm.

A tree that is firmly rooted can withstand the storms that threaten it. Although we can't see the roots, they are vitally important. When we trust Jesus for our salvation, we are rooted in Him. Every time we choose faith, our roots go deeper. Throughout this study, we've been spending time with the Lord in the Word and in prayer. This is the work we do that no one else gets to see—the hidden part. We've been working on our roots. The more we work on our roots, the stronger our faith becomes. When we're rooted in Him, we stand firm. We choose to stand firm—to be unwavering in our faith when we're tempted to fear or worry.

> Therefore as you have received Christ Jesus the Lord,
> so walk in Him, having been firmly rooted and now
> being built up in Him and established in your faith,
> just as you were instructed, and overflowing with gratitude.
> —Colossians 2:6–7

We received Jesus by faith, now we are to keep walking in Him by choosing faith each step of the way. As our roots grow, we will not just see the storms and trials in life, we'll be able to see God moving in our storms and trials. Each time we choose to walk by faith and obey His commands, we are being built up in Him. Our roots are deep and strong because we have followed His instructions. We are established and secure. We are firmly rooted in Him; therefore, we can refuse to go back to our old habits of fear and worry. When we realize this, we will overflow with gratitude. Storms will try to up-root us, but in Christ we "will be like a tree firmly planted by streams of water, which yields its fruit in its season and its leaf does not wither" (Psalm 1:3).

Romans 8:28 reminds us that "God causes all things to work together for good to those who love God, to those who are called according to His purpose." Everything that has happened, is happening, or will happen, can be used for His glory and for our good. In some varieties of mustard plants, every part is edible—nothing gets wasted. Every part of our faith journey will be used by God for His good purposes! Stand firm, rooted in Him—He is faithful to complete the good work He has begun in you! (Philippians 1:6).

## DAY 1

When the seed of faith takes root, we'll discover that we're firmly grounded in the Lord. What a sweet place to be!

Write out our memory verse, Psalm 112:7.

Why will this person not fear adversity?

What does it mean to be steadfast?

Pray and ask the Holy Spirit to guide you as you read Luke 6:46–49. According to verse 46, what does God require of us?

If we are claiming to belong to the Lord, then we should be living a life that reflects Him. How does your life look? God blesses those who live obedient lives. This doesn't mean we have to live *perfect* lives! In verse 48 we get a picture of the person who lives in obedience. What do you observe?

What happened when the rain and floods came? Why?

When we trust in the Lord, we're on solid ground. Ask the Lord to examine your heart and show you if there are areas of disobedience in your life. Confess your disobedience and choose to walk in His ways. Ask Him to firmly root you in Him so you can stand firm when the floods come.

## DAY 2

Pray and ask the Holy Spirit to teach you as you read and meditate on Psalm 112.

Who is blessed in verse 1?

_____

_____

What are the characteristics of the upright in verses 4–5?

_____

_____

In verse 6, we see that this blessed one will never be shaken. Have you ever felt shaken? What does this verse mean?

_____

_____

The world around us might come undone; but when we are steadfast in the Lord, nothing can shake us spiritually. This fact helps us not to fear the evil tidings in verse 7.

What do you notice about the heart in verse 8?

_____

_____

Pray through this psalm and commit your ways to the Lord.

## DAY 3

Read and meditate on Psalm 40. Invite the Holy Spirit to teach you.

In verse 1, how did David wait for the Lord?

_____

_____

In this day and age, we don't like to wait at all. However, God grows our faith while we wait on Him. A sweet 3-year-old boy once told me that being patient means waiting happily. Are you happily waiting on the Lord?

_____

_____

What did God do for David in verse 2?

_____

_____

As we go through challenges, it often feels as if we are in the pit! But when we keep seeking Him, He is faithful to pull us out and set our feet upon the rock.

In verse 6, there are things God does not desire from us. What are they?

_____

_____

In verse 8, what *does* God desire from us?

_____

_____

In verses 11–17, David brought a new problem before the Lord. It's good for us to remember that David's life was not smooth and easy. What does David declare in verse 11?

_____

_____

_____

This can be your declaration as well! Spend time praying through this psalm.

## DAY 4

In spite of our trials and fears, we can stand firm and wait for the Lord to show up.

Read Exodus 14:1–14.

The Israelites were on their way to freedom . . . and then in verse 10 they looked back. What did they see?

_____

_____

What did they do in verses 11–12?

_____

_____

The Israelites weren't dealing very well with the situation! Imagine how Moses must have felt in that moment. The Egyptians were chasing them down, and all of Israel was angry with him. Not a good day! But Moses did exactly what he told the people to do. What did he say in verses 13–14?

_____

_____

Standing firm means waiting confidently! The Lord always shows up! We know the rest of the story; the Lord did indeed deliver them.

In the New Testament, we read about the apostle Paul, who led many to Christ. He suffered more than we could probably imagine. Read 2 Corinthians 11:23–29 to get an idea of what he endured for the sake of Christ. List what Paul experienced.

_____

_____

Paul's foundation was firm. He did not waver from the call of the Lord. He persevered, and he stood firm.

Write out 2 Corinthians 12:9–10.

_____

_____

_____

_____

_____

Paul was declaring that in his greatest weakness, he found the greatest strength! Let Christ be your strength in your worries and challenges. We're not trying to get to a place in life where we're strong enough to handle any disaster. We're trying to grow our faith in the One who will be our strength—the One who can handle any disaster! Spend time in prayer reflecting on your response to the storms and challenges of life. Ask Him to grow that steadfast spirit within you.

## DAY 5

Standing firm is a choice. We can't win the battle if we're not firmly planted. Pray and ask the Holy Spirit to teach you as you read through the following verses.

Read Galatians 5:1. In Christ we have freedom. What are we told to do in this verse?

_____

_____

_____

Read Ephesians 6:10–17. Where do we get our strength?

_____

_____

_____

What are we told to do in verse 11? Why?

_____

_____

_____

According to Paul, "Our struggle is not against flesh and blood, but against the rulers, against the authorities, against the powers of this dark world and against the spiritual forces of evil in the heavenly realms" (Ephesians 6:12, NIV). In other words, the battle is against Satan and his demons. Therefore, according to verse 13, what should we do?

_____

_____

_____

Verses 14–17 list the armor of God. List each piece and describe its purpose.

_____

_____

_____

_____

_____

How many times in these passages did Paul tell us to stand firm?

_____

_____

Standing firm is the only way to do battle!

Read 1 Peter 5:8–9.

What are we to do in verse 8? Why?

_____

_____

How do we do that, according to verse 9?

_____

_____

With your list of fears, spend time with the Lord declaring that you will choose to be steadfast in the Lord—no matter what may come. This is the safest place.

# TELL OTHERS

## WEEK 12

We've made it to the final week of our study! I know that, as you have sought the Lord, He has done good things in you! One final interesting fact about the mustard seed—did you know the mustard seed, and the mustard plant, have healing properties? Faith brings healing in our lives. A tiny seed of faith can change our course of life from a fear-filled worrier to a faith-filled warrior!

In Mark 5:1–20 we read the story of Jesus setting free a man possessed by many demons. He couldn't even be shackled because no one was strong enough to subdue him. He was isolated and in desperate need of help. This man had never met Jesus before, yet the demons in him knew exactly who Jesus was—the Son of the Most High God. Jesus commanded the demons to go and sent them into a herd of swine. Immediately, this man's life was transformed by the power of Jesus. In verse 15, we see that "They came to Jesus and observed the man who had been demon-possessed sitting down, clothed and in his right mind, the very man who had had the 'legion'; and they became frightened." The man was radically different, and the people noticed. The man suddenly understood the power of Jesus and implored Jesus to let him follow Him.

> And He did not let him, but He said to him, "Go home to your people and report to them what great things the Lord has done for you, and how He had mercy on you." And he went away and began to proclaim in Decapolis what great things Jesus had done for him; and everyone was amazed.
>
> —Mark 5:19–20

A thankful heart will not be silent. What has the Lord done for you as you've worked through your fears and worries? It is good to boast about the Lord's goodness and faithfulness. When we do so, we're planting seeds of faith in someone else's garden! You have a testimony, a story of your salvation. You are the only one who gets to tell that story because it is uniquely yours. You've had prayers answered by the Lord during the last 12 weeks. When you share those stories with others, you have the power of the Holy Spirit to bring them hope! I trust that, during this time, your heart has been changed as well. You're stronger in your relationship with Him, and your little seed of faith has sprouted, grown, and bloomed. Now it's time to bear fruit—and plant seeds for those around you.

> Come and hear, all who fear God,
>
> And I will tell of what He has done for my soul.
>
> —Psalm 66:16

To tell others about His work in our lives magnifies the Lord. Testimonies remind us that the same power that rose Jesus from the grave is alive and at work within us. Not only do testimonies encourage and bring hope, they also glorify God! The way we live our lives testifies to the Lord's faithfulness and goodness. As you move from fear to faith, others will notice that you're not responding to the pressures of life in the ways you did before. Tell them what the Lord has done for you!

> Let your light shine before men in such a way
>
> that they may see your good works,
>
> and glorify your Father who is in heaven.
>
> —Matthew 5:16

## DAY 1

That little seed of faith has grown and is now bearing fruit. We bear fruit by living obedient lives (which we've been doing through this study) and planting seeds of faith into those around us. Telling others what Jesus has done in our lives is the way to plant those seeds.

Write out our last memory verses, Matthew 28:19–20.

_____

_____

_____

_____

In those verses, what does Jesus call us to do?

_____

_____

_____

Pray and ask the Holy Spirit to teach you as you read 1 Corinthians 3:6–9. What is Paul saying in this passage?

_____

_____

_____

Each of us has a part to play. We might be planting seeds, or we might be watering seeds that someone else has planted, but we should be doing something!

Who does Paul say we are in verse 9?

_____

_____

_____

We are called to work together in harmony. Growing His kingdom is not a competition; we are on the same team. Spend time thanking Him that you're a part of His team, and ask Him what He wants you to do for His kingdom.

# DAY 2

Pray and ask the Holy Spirit to teach you as you read and paraphrase the following verses.

Psalm 35:28

_____

_____

_____

Psalm 40:9–10

_____

_____

_____

Psalm 71:15–18

_____

_____

_____

Matthew 10:32

_____

_____

_____

Luke 8:39

_____

_____

_____

1 Peter 3:15

_____

_____

_____

What is the common theme of all these verses?

_____

_____

_____

It's so important to share with others what the Lord has done in your life! This is why we were put here on earth: to share the love of Christ with a dying world, to encourage and edify the body of Christ, and to glorify and magnify God! Spend time in prayer and commit to the Lord your desire to tell others about Him. Ask Him to give you opportunities to share.

# DAY 3

Looking at your list of fears and worries, are there any you can cross off that no longer cause you fear?

_____

_____

_____

_____

Why do you no longer fear them?

_____

_____

Are there any that haven't gone away completely, but no longer have the same power over you?

_____

_____

God is doing a work in you! Remember, it isn't about removing all your fears at once. It's about growing your faith—*one* fear, *one* worry, *one* struggle at a time.

Write out Philippians 1:6.

_____

_____

_____

God isn't done with you yet! He has so much more in store for you. Spend some time with the Lord right now, worshiping and thanking Him for His faithfulness to you.

If you're still struggling with your fears and worries, do not be discouraged! Remember, it's a process. It takes time to renew our minds and change from our old ways of thinking. God has neither forgotten you nor failed you. This is your chance to stand firm and wait happily!

Write out the following verses. Underline the command and double underline God's promise.

Isaiah 40:31

_____

_____

_____

Isaiah 41:13

_____

_____

_____

Make these verses your prayer to the Lord. He will be faithful to answer them!

## DAY 4

Ask the Holy Spirit to guide you as you read and meditate on Psalm 37. This is a psalm about moving beyond worry to trusting the Lord. According to this psalm, what should not cause us worry or fret?

_____

_____

_____

What are we called to do in verse 3?

_____

_____

Every time we trust in the Lord, we are cultivating faithfulness! Write out verse 4.

_____

_____

_____

_____

What does it mean to "delight yourself in the Lord"?

_____

_____

What does it mean that He will give you the desires of your heart?

_____

_____

In verse 5 David tells us how to delight in the Lord. What are we instructed to do?

This psalm is filled with instructions of how to commit your way to the Lord. Write down as many as you can find.

Next, write down how God will respond to our faithfulness—these are His promises.

Spend time praying and declaring to God that—instead of worrying—you will continue to trust in Him and obey Him.

## DAY 5

What specifically has God done for you over the course of our study? Has He changed your perspective? Has He given you peace in a fearful situation? Has He answered a specific prayer? Has He spoken to you through His Word?

Write out a letter of thanks to the Lord for what He has done.

_____

_____

_____

_____

_____

_____

_____

_____

_____

_____

_____

You are well on your way from fear to faith. Keep reviewing what you've learned and renewing your mind in His Word, and He will continue to grow that tree of faith!

# WRAP UP

What a journey we've taken! I hope this study has encouraged your heart. I trust that God has drawn you closer to Him as you've pursued Him, seeking to leave your fears and worries behind. Your little seed of faith has grown, as you've moved from fear to faith. What victory that is! I remember a dear pastor who once said, "You are either in a storm right now, you have just come out of one, or you are about to head into one." Isn't that true?

Even so, when you abide in Him, He will help you continue to **dig out weeds**, **destroy idols** and **thwart lies** that are trying to grow back. If you take your gaze off Him and fall, remember to **look up**, and He will meet you, just as He did when Peter was walking on the water. As you **choose faith** and trust Him, He will keep growing your faith and produce much fruit. **Worship Him** and **thank Him** when you **pray**; this feeds your faith. **Know who you are**—you are a masterpiece to Him. **Know His Word**—it's the only way to renew your mind. Dig in your heels and **stand firm**; you are anchored to the Rock! Magnify and glorify the Lord—**tell others** what He has done in you. The storms—and the fears that go along with them—will come, but you know what to do . . .

When I am afraid,

I will put my trust in You.

—Psalm 56:3

# ACKNOWLEDGMENTS

From Fear to Faith came together with the hands,
minds, and hearts of many people!

Renee Garrick—I confess I was fearful of the editing
process! Thank you for your discernment in the details
and the grace-filled way you sharpened the study!

Greg Jackson—thank you for bringing a whole new dimension to
this study with color and design. You have brought it to life!

Josiah Bondy—it has been a delight to work with you!
Thank you for your expertise and patience in working with
someone who prefers to run from the camera!

Jeanne, Sheila, Candi, and Renee—you sharpen, encourage, and inspire
me to know Him more! Thank you for pouring into those around
you with this message of the hope of moving from fear to faith!

David, Emma, Luke, Lily, and Elijah—thank you for cheering me
on, for coming to my rescue with all my computer challenges,
and for letting me spend a lot of time encouraging others. May
the Lord bless you beyond measure! I love you so much!

Brett and Sheila Waldman at TRISTAN Publishing—I had no idea this
would be so much fun. It has been an adventure! Woo-hoo!! Thank you
for stepping out in faith, believing in me, encouraging me, and praying
for me. I will always cherish our time together—love you, friends!

Most of all I want to thank Jesus for moving me from fear to faith. My garden
did not grow overnight. You have been faithful and patient each step of the
way. What a glorious adventure it has been with You! "Now to Him who is
able to do far more abundantly beyond all that we ask or think, according
to the power that works within us, to Him be the glory in the church and in
Christ Jesus to all generations forever and ever. Amen." Ephesians 3:20–21

For additional encouragement and blessing, be sure to check out
From Fear to Faith at www.TRISTANpublishing.com.

# BIO

Julie has been married to her better half, David, since 1995. They met on a roller coaster, became engaged on that same roller coaster a year later, and have determined that marriage is a lot like a roller coaster. Their favorite phrase is, "It's an adventure!" Julie is a mom to three kids: Emma, Lily, and Elijah. She and David are super excited about adding son-in-law Luke to the family. Julie ministered to kids for 20 years as an early-childhood educator before transitioning to adult ministry. She is a discipleship and biblical counselor, an author of Bible studies, and a teacher in a variety of settings. Julie loves spending time with family and friends, bringing the hope of Jesus to the broken, and encouraging others in their faith.

# WEEKLY MEMORY VERSES

### PSALM 56:3

When I am afraid,
I will put my trust in You.

### PSALM 121:1-2

I will lift up my eyes to the mountains;
From where shall my help come?
My help comes from the Lord,
Who made heaven and earth.

### HEBREWS 11:6

And without faith it is impossible
to please Him, for he who comes to God
must believe that He is and that He is a
rewarder of those who seek Him.

### PSALM 95:6

Come, let us worship and bow down,
Let us kneel before the Lord our Maker.

### DEUTERONOMY 6:5

You shall love the Lord your God
with all your heart and with all your
soul and with all your might.

### 2 CORINTHIANS 5:17

Therefore if anyone is in Christ, he is a
new creature; the old things passed away;
behold, new things have come.

### 1 THESSALONIANS 5:16-18

Rejoice always; pray without ceasing;
in everything give thanks; for this is
God's will for you in Christ Jesus.

### 2 CHRONICLES 7:14 (NIV)

If my people, who are called by my name,
will humble themselves and pray and seek
my face and turn from their wicked ways,
then I will hear from heaven, and I will
forgive their sin and will heal their land.

### JOHN 8:32 (NIV)

Then you will know the truth,
and the truth will set you free.

### PSALM 119:165

Those who love Your law have great peace,
And nothing causes them to stumble.

### PSALM 112:7

He will not fear evil tidings;
His heart is steadfast,
trusting in the Lord.

### MATTHEW 28:19-20

Go therefore and make disciples
of all the nations, baptizing them
in the name of the Father and the Son
and the Holy Spirit, teaching them
to observe all that I commanded you;
and lo, I am with you always,
even to the end of the age.

# NOTES